NONNA
And Other Italian Stories

Memoirs of a young woman; my 18 years of memories in a special Italian family

*"alla **famiglia**"*

LUCY CORDERO

BALBOA.PRESS
A DIVISION OF HAY HOUSE

Balboa Press books may be ordered through booksellers or by contacting:

Balboa Press
A Division of Hay House
1663 Liberty Drive
Bloomington, IN 47403
www.balboapress.com
844-682-1282

Because of the dynamic nature of the Internet, any web addresses or
links contained in this book may have changed since publication and
may no longer be valid. The views expressed in this work are solely those
of the author and do not necessarily reflect the views of the publisher,
and the publisher hereby disclaims any responsibility for them.

The author of this book does not dispense medical advice or prescribe the use
of any technique as a form of treatment for physical, emotional, or medical
problems without the advice of a physician, either directly or indirectly. The
intent of the author is only to offer information of a general nature to help
you in your quest for emotional and spiritual well-being. In the event you use
any of the information in this book for yourself, which is your constitutional
right, the author and the publisher assume no responsibility for your actions.

Any people depicted in stock imagery provided by Getty Images are
models, and such images are being used for illustrative purposes only.
Certain stock imagery © Getty Images.

Print information available on the last page.

ISBN: 978-1-9822-5662-3 (sc)
ISBN: 978-1-9822-5663-0 (e)

Balboa Press rev. date: 10/27/2020

DEDICATION

My children, Jennifer and Michael and my grandson, Vincent, and for the descendants of grandmother Anita, and my in laws, Marie and Jim, her mother, Anita, (Nonna) and her sisters, Josephine, (Auntie Jo) and Anna (Aunt Dippy), cousin Johnny

On my beloved father-in-law's side, Jim, (Pop-Pop), his siblings, Uncles Joe, Neil, Sal, Ralph, Aunts, Lucy, Agnes, Anna, my brother-in-law, Frank, and cousins, Gerry and Angela.

This personal memoire is a testimony to the profound impact that a wonderful family can have on an impressionable young woman who was at crossroad between sweet teenage innocence and womanhood. The years with these relatives who came from another culture and time, opened up a new world of beautiful experiences, and loving memories. How lucky was I to spend special celebrations, ordinary family time where I came into my own mature understanding about the true meaning of life and happiness.

THE BEST WAY TO READ THIS BOOK IS WHILE THERE'S A POT OF GRAVY AND MEATBALLS SIMMERING ON THE STOVE, AND DRINKING A GLASS OF WINE, AS A RECORD OF DEAN MARTIN SINGING "AMORE" IS PLAYING ON THE VICTROLA.

CONTENTS

CHAPTER 1

MEET NONNA

IN 1966 NONNA was already in her 70's, and she was then and until her death in 1998 at age 96, she was and will forever be, the quintessential Italian grandmother. She was the typical old-world Nonna of the 1930, 50's and 60's who simply adapted her previous life from old world Larino Italy to New York.

She was approximately four feet nothing. It is universally known, that first generations Italian grandmother, easily recognized as a genuine Nonna, (as opposed to second or third generation grandmothers,) are typically short and round or square shaped. Nonna was a short squat box shaped lady with plain features, sagging breasts and large waist, blessed with with exquisite culinary skills.

NONNA wore black tied up shoes which had the heels worn down on the instep so she tilted when she walked to and from the kitchen to the dining room. She could afford new shoes, but no, the ones she wore everyday for the 15 years I knew her, were serviceable even if they were worn down.

Picture this, hair cut short boy style instead of the proverbial bun, a square flat face, which never required make up expect face powder for a wedding or funeral. Her thin cotton shift dress usually thread-bare, with short sleeves, and although she could easily afford a new dress, she wore her house dress until it too, was worn out and then became a cleaning rag. Over her home-made shift dress, she always wore a cotton bib apron or sometimes a cook's white duck tie back apron where she tucked a dish cloth to wipe her hands as she cooked or washed dishes. If she had company visiting or eating with the family, she took the apron off as company was a formal occasion. She preferred aprons with pockets but her shift usually had a pocket to put doodads and loose change. Nonna was height challenged in comparison to everyone in the family, even shorter than her grandchildren after they reached the age of 10. Her grandsons towered over her and she had to stretch up on her tip toes to kiss them.

To have had the privilege to be a guest at Nonna's table was an honor. To an impressionable sixteen-year-old girlfriend of a revered Italian grandson, (and Nonna's favorite (as was explained to me by my ex,) is now a special and sacred memory. The sun and the moon rose in Nonna' grandchildren, but her eldest grandchild was not denied any delicacy he wanted at any time of the day or night.

When I met Nonna for the first time in 1966, I was mesmerized and enchanted as it was almost 8 PM and she was bubbling over with joy at the sight of her grandson. Of course, as is the Italian custom, the first thing she asked me, is was if I was hungry and I would I want something to eat. Without a moment's hesitation, the favorite grandson tells her he wants spaghetti with marinara gravy, (remember it is always gravy, not sauce!) Nonna looks pleadingly at her grandson so as to say, "ma, Jimmy, itsa late, and I hefta to cooka the gravy now? Are you sure you wanna spaghetti now?" My boyfriend replies, "Nonna PULEEZE, I'm your favorite grandson, and I love to have your marinara so you want me to be happy right?"

Needless to say, she dutifully went into the kitchen to cook the homegrown tomatoes, simmering it with fresh basil and sugar, and to this day 50 years later, the gravy was the very best I have ever tasted! At that moment, I wanted Nonna to be my grandmother, and for 18 years I was in the family, I adopted her as my own grandmother.

CHAPTER 2

NONNA GOES SHOPPING AT THE FLEA MARKET

N ONNA WAS A force to be reckoned with when it came to shopping, especially for food. Sometimes it fell to me to take Nonna shopping when I visited her. So little Nonna would change her house dress for a nicer but very much the same, cotton shift dress. She put on her better special occasion black tie-up well heed shoes, and grabbed her large black handbag with the chrome clasp. She clutched that bag, close to her body to protect the little fabric money pouch with another clasp, where her precisely counted coins and bills. I recall she was pretty darn cute, and so happy to be on the outing of the month.

In 1967, the best place for bargains near her Westbury home was in Hicksville, Hew York, at the Farmer's Market. I have to admit it was a terrific place to shop for all kinds of commodities, that included clothes, home décor, toys, shoes including nonna shoes, and of course food of several ethnic origins, native to a diverse population, and particularly of old world Italian nonnas. The highlight of the shopping spree was to the two or three Italian specialty booths, where there were various large roped cheese blocks and dried sausages hanging over the tall glass counter, similar to any respected Italian deli. The refrigerated glass enclosed display of most Italian cold meats, to include but not limited to different hams, and the best and freshest Salami, Prosciutto, Mortadella, Capicola, Pancetta, Bresaola, etc. The mozzarella was always fresh and part of the essential shopping items.

It was at these counters where little Nonna made her food selections to the counter men who knew her well, addressing her as Nonna, as she stretched up on her toes to point to the specific items she wanted to taste before she bought anything. They were very respectful towards her; the deli counterman man would slice up the meats and cheeses and they would walk around to the end of the counter to give Nonna the tasting pieces to get her approval before getting permission to slice up the meat to her exact specifications. This type of service was repeated at the butcher counter and at the vegetable booth and the bakery booth. What a treat to observe the master shopper at work procuring her treasures of food for her family. Her children and grandchildren inherited this refined appetite for Italian specialties and will go to several specialty vendors to find the exact nonna-worthy cuts of meats. Next stop was the flea market bakery for fresh Italian bread and pignole cookies.

The best part of the shopping day was to bring the fresh cold cuts, fresh tomatoes, and fresh soft Italian bread, a little wine and to sit down to a delicious lunch with Nonna and Auntie Jo. And later in the day, there would be a scrumptious dinner of carefully prepared courses to include but not limited to fresh salad, (dandelion was special), home-made soup, then for the entre of a roast, or home-made pasta dish. Well, there isn't enough space and time to name all the wonderful dishes served with love to the growing family she created over her 80 years of family life of love.

CHAPTER 3

MORE NONNA TRIVIA

THERE ARE SO many other small but special Nonna habits and memorable things she always did everyday of her life. There's a memory of Nonna's stubby fingers being in perpetual motion with a task related to food.

There was her pantry filled with home grown tomatoes in mason jars she boiled up and then put up for future gravy dishes. You could taste the freshness of the ripe tomatoes and fresh basil in every jar poured out for the family's authentic Italian dinner. Earlier you recall, I discussed the fresh marinara gravy that has been carefully replicated by her favorite grandson, (my former husband) and he passed down to my son and will be passed down to her great-great grandson.

Sometimes she served the gravy with her own home-made pasta for a really special treat.

Nonna's pantry included many sized of jars sealed in the height of freshness, like the vegetarian pasta and bean soup otherwise known as pasta fagioli with Ditalini, a tiny, tube-shaped pasta. She put up roasted red pepper in olive oil vinegar, artichoke hearts, and all kinds of Italian delicacies, She would store the various beans and pasta in their separate jars which we found on the shelf after her death. The jars would be marked on surgical tape strips written in Italian. Finding those jars in her pantry would always bring back fond memories. She used to save thin cotton twine she saved from bakery boxes she wound up in little balls for use to wrap chunks of pork fat, or Rolled Beef or pork Braciole or tied bunches of fresh parsley and basil, which she hung up to dry.

Most old world nonnas made their own pasta, which was kneaded and rolled out or pinched into little pope hats, cappelletti, pappardelle, my favorite was fusilli. Sometimes her bed had linen table clothes laid carefully on her bed so the pasta could dry out and carefully wrapped up with string, or put up in glass jars. How much work she put into the creation of specialty pasta dishes, we never really appreciated.

Nonna will live forever in real and tangible memories we can see and smell and eat and while her descendants carry on her cherished cooking traditions. The expression of Nonna's maternal love is just as important the minds and memories of her family, as any modern-day grandmother. She may not have been remembered for anything outside of her family life, but her achievement of cultivating respect and admiration from her family is what she will be remembered for by anyone who knew her. Nonna's contribution to the world, would be the preservation of a wonderful family history of the past of traditional celebrations and gatherings. Anyone invited to her table to share a meal, would cherish the experience. We will remember her sitting at a small kitchen table, on a plastic padded metal framed 1960's style chair, with a big bowl in front of her when she was using an ancient cutting board, cutting up a piece of meat she intended to filet. Before putting a roast, she put it in her favorite roasting pan, that was tenderly scrubbed after dinner for many years of use. Or I can remember her, stuffing squid for a fish pasta dinner for Christmas eve. Sometimes she would pour a little glass juice glass with some sweet red wine, and sip it while her hands kept busy with food preparations.

Here's to NONNA, the best grandmother in the whole world! Cent'Anni!, Ti vogliama bene!

MY FORMER HUSBAND'S
SECOND GENERATION

*New York City family and my father-in-law Jim,
(aka Pop Pop) is the fellow on the top right and my
grandson's great grandfather and namesake*

CHAPTER 4

MORE ITALIAN FAMILY GATHERING MEMORIES

"ALLA FAMIGLIA" Cosmo Casterini, 1987 MOONSTRUCK,

1980 FATSO, Domonick DiPaolo kitchen at the wake of cousin Sal

1990 GOODFELLAS, scene in Paulie's backyard barbeque

E VERYONE KNOWS THAT Italian celebrations are something special and ethnically different than other groups of people as long as there are one or two or three generation immigrants still alive to carry on traditions.

Among my ex-husbands family, on his father's side, the 18 years of sharing my early courting and marriage with the most wonderful people I have ever know, were a large amount of "real New Yok" Italian relatives.

There were 8 siblings born of first generation immigrants of Italian people from Calabria who lived in Queens New York. My father-in-law had 4 brothers and three sisters making the family of 8 children fully assimilated to settle in Brooklyn and Queens New York, and remained close to one another throughout their lives.

Those 8 children married and when I came into the family, these sixteen people had two children each, (two of them had three kids) bringing the third generation of cousin count to 18, and this was the family that celebrated weddings and funerals, a total of 34 people with whom life was celebrated. Those of us cousins who were married also had children and then the fourth generation included my own two children. They, my kids, still cherish fond memories of all these relatives from their early childhood memories before me and my husband split up and I sometimes miss these wonderful in-laws-more than my own relatives.

CHAPTER 5

THE BARBEQUE FOOD OF NEW YORK ITALIANS

A BARBEQUE ITALIAN STYLE

F ORGET ABOUT HOT dogs and hamburgers as being the main course for the 30, plus a few cousin's boyfriends or girlfriends and other close relatives, gathered together at an Italian family barbeque held in the backyard of my ex-father-in-law's home. The time in history was mid 1960's before my marriage and then continued into the early 1970's.

The barbeque would be sometimes in other relative's backyard, even in small Queens or Brooklyn backyards. My boyfriend's parents lived on Long Island, so this was the preferred location for a more suitable site so many people to cook and eat a ton of food. The traveling relatives all came with food and drinks and bread and boxes of food and the teenage boys carted them to the back. They also brought large insulated coolers for beer and soda and wine bottles. Of course, there were lots of bakery grade, tied white pastry boxes from the best city bakeries, for after dinner coffee and expresso.

The older uncles wore white sleeveless t-shirts my son calls "wife beater" undershirts. Then they would wear ironed button-down short- sleeve cotton shirts which they would take off as the sun grew hotter. The aunts wore cotton shift dresses, with cobbler aprons to protect their dresses whlle they cooked or served food or washed dishes. They also wore open black or white leather buckled sandals with stockings! Only my mother-in-law and the youngest aunt wore pants or shorts. My father-in-law was the main cook and you could always wear a kitchen towel tucked into his belt and another one over his shoulder and a big clean handkerchief tucked into his pocket used to wipe the proliferation of beads of sweat forming on his forehead from the high heat over the sausage and onions and peppers on the grill, which he tended to with loving care.

There were make shift picnic tables, covered with plastic oil fabric or starched cloth linen table clothes, a couple of the picnic tables also had plastic sun fringed umbrellas for the older folks to protect them from the sun. The seating was a hodge podge of chairs, including webbed aluminum framed lawn chairs, and wood kitchen table chairs or folding metal chairs. There were always at least two smaller tables set up for pinochle and polka card games played for nickles and dimes. Of course, at the back of the yard there is a bocce ball set up and/or a horse shoe track for the uncles and teenage boys.

There were a few small kitchen tables up against the house so that electricity could be provided to the two large electric burners used for cooking pots and pans, boiling water for corn, heating up gravy and sautéing peppers and onions and mushrooms.

Also, the outlets for electricity was required for the large Victrola where long playing albums were stacked up for Italian crooner records of Jimmy Roselli, Louie Prima, Dean Martin, Jerry Vale and more. This music was as much as the fabric of the family gatherings of a generation of New Yorkers from the 1940's, 50's and

60's as the marathon card games, the bocce and horse shoe contests.

The menu is of course the most important part of the day which was thoroughly discussed and planned prior to the event.

The main barbeque was constructed with concrete blocks with a large stainless-steel grate at two levels, and on the ground was a metal and iron rack tray for charcoal briquettes, where bags of charcoal was fed into the fire pit all day long. Around the same main concrete barbeque, were two or three smaller old1960 vintage dome top metal leg grilling barbeques. These cooking stations were manned by the older men or one of the women, to ensure proper cooking of various meat items. There was a large black cast iron frying pan for the sausage, onions and pepper sandwiches to be served on fresh Italian bread brought in from Brooklyn. There were onions sautéing and barbeque chicken and pork spare ribs, stuffed portabella mushrooms, plain sausage, and then another grill for hamburgers and hot dog for the teenagers and kids.

On the stove there was corn on the cobb and then a pot of gravy in case someone wanted tomatos on their sandwiches, or to dip their bread in as an antipasto with provolone cheese and sweet and hot and pepperoni dried sausage, prosciutto, capicola, salami, etc. Of course, there was the traditional Italian style potato and macaroni and penne cold salads. The choices of food to eat was seemingly endless and everyone would be able to satisfy their taste while engaging in yard games, card playing, gossiping and laughing by sharing memories of older times.

As already mentioned, the desserts are unlike anything you get at most American barbeques, so suffice to say the heavenly Italian fancy pastries the names of which t I could never pronounce are, and will always be a cherished family tradition. The consumption of these delicacies were the final treat and delightful highlight of the day. The fresh bakery pastries included but not limited to cannoli, sfogliatella, castagnole, biscotti, etc. Sometimes there was an Italian cheese cake and chiacchiere with white powdered sugar sprinkled on top.

These dessert items were served with fresh coffee and expresso, with some sambuca liquor, for the piece de reisistance. This course was the final course of food for the end of a perfect day of love.

This menu plus more, was also typical food for

weddings, (although the antipasto and penne and salad was much more elaborate,) for weddings, baptisms, and funerals.

Good food is the essence of Italian life, like air for breath. Food shows us how love is expressed, the meal ties and binds us together as a family. It the raison d'etre for Italians, and anyone who has had the privilege of sharing meals within a close family unit, could not compare the experience to other relationships since the food was the glue that held us together, It defined what we can still smell and imagine today of a time when we visited grandparents, and a generation old world Italian relatives.

Those cherished people are gone now, except the husband of the youngest sister, and the wife of the youngest brother, who are still alive. However, the memory of their laughing and smothering hugs and kisses is a sweet experience for me. Hopefully, this family of over a hundred relations, took many photographs of the people with whom they shared these cherished memories so that we will forever remember them and who we hope to see in another life, please God.

CHAPTER 6

OUR BELOVED POP POP (AKA JIM)

M Y FORMER FATHER-IN-LAW, Jim, was the third son of an Italian immigrant came to New York, early in the late 1800's to raise his 8 children

My father-in-law always went by the name, Jimmy, although that wasn't his real name. I am making an educated guess that he was born in New York city around 1917. Around the 1950's his siblings mostly settled in Glendale Queens and Brooklyn to raise their own families, living in close proximity to one another thereby ensuring the continuance of their Italian family traditions. He was the third of 8 children, 5 brothers and 3 sisters. In his youth he bore a strong resemblance to Billy Halop, of the 1938 Dead End Kids fame. He was handsome and brash and was respected and cherished by his 7 siblings because he had dropped out of school to work to help his parents to support the large family during the depression. I believe he said he shined shoes during the depression. He was drafted to serve in World War II in Europe and sent his money home. He once told me a story about how the troops in Europe hated General Patton for slapping an enlisted soldier who had resorted to claiming battle fatigue rather than going back to the front. He was awarded several medals which have passed down to his son, (my ex,) and now to his youngest grandson, my son, Mike. He had a quick and sometimes violent temper with a touch of bully tendencies. Rarely, he could be cruel towards his wife and children, could be very intimidating at times, but his bad moods were short-lived and his natural amiable self would return. He was intentionally sarcastic when he wanted to make a point, but also funny and charming whenever his extended family and his grandchildren were around.

In the 1950's, Jim worked for the Pennsylvania Railroad out of Grand and he and Marie (Nonna's second daughter mentioned in the beginning of this book), married in May of 1947. There as a bit of a scandal about Marie and Jim, because at the time of Jim and her' premarital courting, Marie had already been engaged to a sailor, who was her family's preferred suitor. So when Marie accepted a proposal of marriage to Jim, her family was outraged.

There's a funny but poignant family story about my in-laws, In 1972, we the children of Jim and Marie, decided to throw our parents a 25th wedding anniversary with all the 16 aunts and uncles and 40 cousins at a catered affair in a Knights of Columbus Hall. This then, was the reason for Marie's family extreme consternation at the rushed marriage of Marie to Jim. They stayed married for over 40 years, a contentious marriage, but devoted to one another until Jim's death in the 90's.

He had been injured on his railroad job, (never knew what his job was) that left him with a permanent back disability, for which he received a disability pension. He was only in his early 40's when he was forced to retire and had to become the "house husband" of the 1960's while his wife, Marie went to work full time to help raise the three children. By that time the family moved from Queens to Long Island in the beginning of the 1960's. That is where I met my future brother-in-law in 6th grade, and them my future husband, in 1965. By 1966, Jimmy and I were boyfriend and girlfriend, and my immersion into the family began, first with Nonna and then my-father-in laws side.

I believe there were 40 children among his siblings and their children and his own three children. He loved them all but he had his favorites and they knew who they were because he made it so obvious. One of the eldest male nephews was a large 6 foot plus, but affable and loveable cousin was known as Gerry. This beautiful young man died when he was a young father of two and it broke our hearts. Then one of his sister's daughter, Suzanne, who was another favored niece. over all other second generation children, right up to her own marriage in the early 70's. The last favorite niece was the youngest daughter of his youngest brother, which was Gloria. He gushed over her every time we had a family affair, unabashed by his favoritism for Gloria and to this day she knows what she meant to him. The rest of the cousins learned to accept this unfair preference to all others.

Jim, the father was strict and feared by his children,

but he also encouraged the two boys to be popular, and athletic and funny cut ups, as he was. In 1966, my boyfriend Jimmy and the rest of the children were enjoying a lunch in the backyard, when my sister-in-law, Joanne was ordered to feed the large German Shepard in the caged dog pad area. As she was bending over to put down the dog dish, Jimmy who was playing at target practice with his bee-bee gun, shot her in her buttocks from several yards away! Naturally, she screamed in pain, but her brothers, Jimmy and Frank burst out in raucous laughter at the sight of her grabbing her butt! Yes, they too, both had a streak of cruelty as teenagers when it came to being plain mean to their sister. Since their teenage years, both boys became "misogynists" in the old "Italian" ways of their father's culture. My father-in-law was the kind of husband that would call his wife from the kitchen into the living room to change the TV channel. He was famous for chastising his wife and daughter if either of them forgot to put the salt and pepper on the table. We all dreaded the "Who set the table?" question he sternly asked, especially me if setting the table was my task. My beloved sister-in-law, Joanne's, job was to hand grind the fresh locatelli cheese every Sunday for generous sprinkling over the spaghetti or ziti or fusilli pasta.

Then too, Jim the elder, was ridiculously generous and indulgent when it came to his sons. By the time Jimmy, the minor, graduated high school at 17, his father bought him a 1966 GTO, with 4 speed stick transmission, posi-track suspension, dual glass pack exhausts, and wide oval Mickey Thompson mag wheels. Need I say, a hot car, envied by all his friends, many who challenged him to drag racing in the streets of Selden New York. I learned to drive a 4-speed stick on the floor, by the time I was 18 and only burned out one tranny because like Jimmy, I like to pop the car into gear to leave a black patch of rubber in the street. I'm sure Jimmy helped to pay for that car because he was also working and contributing to the household finances just as his father did when he started earning money, without a shred of resentment by the way.

Jim, the househusband was a "piece of work" as we all affectionately would say. He was meticulous in paperwork of the household finances, and he would sit my mother-in-law down at the kitchen table and instruct her on what to pay, how much, and supervise the recording and filing of all paper work which he saved in bureau drawers for years and years. He perused the supermarket inserts for sales, and made lists for all adults to pick up for the extensive pantry he kept, with lists of how many cans of tomatoes and pasta were on the shelves. His pantry kept in the basement spare room could feed and shelter his family for 3 months at least. He counted every dollar that was spent on food and checked every receipt which he also kept on file for some reason. If you opened the kitchen staples closet which was meticulously organized, you would find on the corner of a shelf, carefully folded used tin foil he saved from his favorite Banquet frozen dinner, chicken pieces with potatoes and corn. He would buy these dinners for himself as lunch and then carefully removed the tin foil before inserting in the over for future use to cover left overs of wrap cold cuts. He saved bakery box strings to wrap up rolled up brajiole (rolled up pork) or some other utilitarian purpose. There was always re-cycled bottles of soda and beer way before that was environmentally required because he needed the nickel return money to buy more soda and beer.

True story, about Jim and sense of economic justice. He was an honest man that would never steal anything, however, one day after we came home from food shopping, I saw him take out a large piece of percorino romano grating cheese from his jacket. I was shocked and I asked him why he did that instead of buying it. He calmly said, the store deli was charging an outrageous amount of money for this item which he felt was why the store deserved the theft to teach them a lesson. He said this with a straight face and I never saw him to that again.

CHAPTER 7

POP POP, THE BEST GRANDFATHER

I N 1972, JIM, hereafter known as POP POP, became
a grandfather to our first daughter, Jennifer, and

his first grandchild. To say that this life event would forever be one of the most important events of his would be an understatement. Jennifer could do no wrong in the eyes of her grandfather for the rest of his life until his death in 1991, and she was 19.

Pop Pop was a devoted and obsessed grandfather who insisted that I retrun to work after maternity leave of 3 months, so that his son, would not have to work two jobs or overtime to support our family. Strangely enough, when his daughter had her own baby, he thought she should not have to return to work, and that her husband needed to be the only breadwinner. I always resented the double standard for me as a new mother and that of my beloved sister-in-law.

True story of his tolerance and indulgence of his revered grand-daughter was the time he was making batches of cooked tomato gravy for pasta, which he would save in 3 lb. ricotta plastic tubs, freezing them for future dinners. We had pasta every Sunday and Wednesday per family tradition and to save money on food. The meatballs were also made in batches about 50 at a time, frozen and put in simmering gravy and which were delicious.

On this particular occasion of making batches

of ricotta tubs filled with cooked gravy, he had put them on the kitchen table without the tops, to cool before putting them in the freezer. Along comes his 18 month old toddler granddaughter and pulls on the table cloth, toppling all the gravy onto the floor, and splattering gravy all over the bottom kitchen cabinets, and the heat registers, etc.

So, when I get home from work, he is sitting in his favorite wing-back chair in front of the TV, sweating and pale faced with a kitchen towel over his shoulder. I didn't see my baby, so I asked him if everything was OK. He said the baby was fine, but she had ruined all the gravy he had been cooking all day. Before I could ask what happened, my mother-in-law walked in the door from her job and she recognized the look on her husband's face, and also asked what happened. He proceeded to tell her to prepare herself for a major mess in the kitchen, and that she had a lot of cleaning up to do. But he had absolutely no annoyance or anger or impatience with his beloved granddaughter who after all, was an angel and not to be chastised.

Another time, I came home from work, only to find him once again, sitting in his chair, ashen faced and exhausted, so again, I asked what was wrong. He replied that Jennifer, the 2 year old baby had been in an accident. I gasped with fear when he quickly informed me she was fine but the car and the neighbors mail box across the street had sustained damage.

He told me that he called his insurance company who immediately came to take an accident report and when the man asked Pop Pop who was driving the care, my father-in-law nonchalantly answers that his grand-daughter was driving. The insurance guy then asks, does she have a license, and Pop Pop said no, and the next question was, how old is your grand-daughter, the answer, she's two.

The story is that Pop-Pop took her food shopping for soda on sale, and when he arrived home, he pulled into the slightly inclined driveway in the front of the garage door. He got out to unload the car of cases of soda, leaving Jennifer in the front seat, (remember there were no seatbelt laws In 1974). As he was taking the case into the garage, Jennifer happily toddled to the steering wheel to play, and released the shifting gear, letting the car go into neutral or reverse, and it rolled down into the street, and hit the neighbor's mail box across the street, splitting the wood post and knocking down the box.

Pop-Pop was shaken up at the potential harm that could have befallen his granddaughter and how he could ever live with himself if she had been hurt. Jennifer was oblivious of course, and once again, he made it clear to all that she was blameless and still a perfect angel no matter what happened to the car of neighbor's mail box.

My in-laws decided to move upstate, to Johnston New York, 5 hours away from where we lived, to help my sister-in-law with her baby and because it would be less expensive for them to live in retirement in a new double wide trailer home on their daughter's property. This was devasting to us as Jennifer was already 3 years old and had been cared for by them since she was 3 months old. Pop-Pop had seriously suggested that we let Jennifer go live with them and we could come a visit her every other weekend. Of course, that wasn't going to happen, and he reluctantly accepted that he would not have Jennifer in his everyday life. It was sad for all of us, but Jennifer was too young to understand. To soften the blow, I traveled the six hours at least once or twice a month until Jennifer was a teenager, and she spend several weeks a year, every summer vacation upstate with her grandparents. She has wonderful memories of those years.

My last Pop-Pop tale was about the hundreds of store studio pictures that he had taken of Jennifer over the years, some with him in them, which he bought every time Sears, or Penny's had a $1.00 portrait sale. Anyone who visited the folks upstate can tell you that Pop-Pops shelves and wall of the trailer were filled with Jennifer portraits, literally, there must have been at least 100+ Sears, Penny's portraits in cheap frames sitting on shelves, on furniture of hanging on the walls in a shrine-like tribute to his favorite grandchild. The other 4 grandchildren also and sadly had to accept that Jennifer was always going to be the "favorite" child, more than his own children, and they all had reluctantly accepted the obvious and somewhat unfair of putting her before the rest of the family.

EPILOGUE

I share these memories of wonderful loving relatives who enriched my life and stored them to my mind and heart. I only hope that my own family will be able to recall the most important times of our lives, those spent with loved ones. These cherished memories are the most important things life has to offer. These stories reflect only 18 years of my life as a young wife and mother. There were tears and sorrow as our marriage came to an end in 1984. But the love and generosity of my former husband's family stayed with me the rest of my life.

Others may be gone but these are the family with whom I had family relationships.

Printed in the United States
By Bookmasters